Through Suffering to Triumph

Through Suffering to Triumph

by
John MacArthur, Jr.

MOODY PRESS
CHICAGO

©1991 by
JOHN F. MACARTHUR, JR.

All rights reserved. No part of this book may be reproduced in any
form without permission in writing from the publisher, except in the
case of brief quotations embodied in critical articles or reviews.

All Scripture quotations, unless noted otherwise, are from the *New
American Standard Bible,* © 1960, 1962, 1963, 1968, 1971, 1972, 1973, 1975,
and 1977 by The Lockman Foundation, and are used by permission.

ISBN: 0-8024-5371-6

1 2 3 4 5 Printing/LC/Year 95 94 93 92 91

Printed in the United States of America

Contents

These Bible studies are taken from messages delivered by Pastor-Teacher John MacArthur, Jr., at Grace Community Church in Sun Valley, California. The recorded messages themselves may be purchased as a series or individually. Please request the current price list by writing to:

"GRACE TO YOU"
P.O. Box 4000
Panorama City, CA 91412

Or call the following toll-free number:
1-800-55-GRACE

1

Glory Through Suffering

Outline

Introduction

Lesson
I.   Christians Are Called to Suffering
II. Christians Are Matured by Suffering
III. Christians Are Brought to Glory Through Suffering
IV. Christians Are Identified with Christ in Their Suffering

Conclusion

Introduction

The theme of 1 Peter 2:21-25 is the suffering of Jesus: "For you have been called for this purpose, since Christ also suffered for you, leaving you an example for you to follow in His steps, who committed no sin, nor was any deceit found in His mouth; and while being reviled, He did not revile in return; while suffering, He uttered no threats, but kept entrusting Himself to Him who judges righteously; and He Himself bore our sins in His body on the cross, that we might die to sin and live to righteousness; for by His wounds you were healed. For you were continually straying like sheep, but now you have returned to the Shepherd and Guardian of your souls."

Peter emphasizes two categories of truth in his first epistle. One is the blessings of the Christian: identification with Christ and its resulting privileges. However, to keep us from assuming that our blessings will result in our being loved and respected by the world, Peter also emphasizes that we will suffer. In fact, 1 Peter clearly shows that those most blessed in the faith suffer the most.

The Christian life is a call to glory through a journey of suffering. That's because those in Christ are inevitably at odds with their culture and society. All Satan-energized systems are actively at odds with the things of Christ. The apostle John said a person can't love both God and the world (1 John 2:15), and James said that "whoever wishes to be a friend of the world makes himself an enemy of God" (James 4:4). That means the Christian is a problem to the society in which he or she lives.

Peter's readers knew both the blessings of life in Christ and the suffering of persecution. They were "scattered throughout Pontus, Galatia, Cappadocia, Asia, and Bithynia" (1 Pet. 1:1). Peter knew of their plight and wrote to comfort them—and everyone else chosen by God for salvation—explaining that along with privilege comes suffering.

Lesson

Peter's model of how to respond to suffering was Jesus Christ. Jesus' attitude toward suffering is to be our attitude.

I. CHRISTIANS ARE CALLED TO SUFFERING

Verse 21 begins with the phrase "For you have been called for this purpose." The connective "for" points back to the last part of verse 20: "If when you do what is right and suffer for it you patiently endure it, this finds favor with God." Christians are to endure suffering because it pleases God. Verse 21 amplifies the idea by stating that Christians are specifically called to suffer.

8

That shouldn't surprise us. Peter had just said that Christians "are a chosen race, a royal priesthood, a holy nation, a people for God's own possession, that [they] may proclaim the excellencies of Him who [called them] out of darkness into His marvelous light" (v. 9). Our dark world resents and is often hostile toward those who represent the Lord Jesus Christ. That resentment and hostility may be felt at certain times and places more than others, but it is always there to some extent.

II. CHRISTIANS ARE MATURED BY SUFFERING

A Christian's call to glory necessitates walking the path of suffering. First Peter 5:10 explains why: "After you have suffered for a little while, the God of all grace, who called you to His eternal glory in Christ, will Himself perfect, confirm, strengthen and establish you." Suffering is God's way of maturing His people spiritually. He is pleased when we patiently endure the suffering that comes our way. Suffering is a part of God's plan to prepare His people for glory.

A. 1 Peter 1:6-7—"You greatly rejoice, even though now for a little while, if necessary, you have been distressed by various trials, that the proof of your faith, being more precious than gold which is perishable, even though tested by fire, may be found to result in praise and glory and honor at the revelation of Jesus Christ." God allows suffering as a validation of our faith. It also produces patience, though patience is a quality we won't need in eternity—there will be no reason for impatience there. Yet beyond those benefits, suffering increases our capacity to praise, glorify, and honor God—and that's something we will use throughout eternity.

B. James 1:2-4—"Consider it all joy, my brethren, when you encounter various trials, knowing that the testing of your faith produces endurance. And let endurance have its perfect result, that you may be perfect and complete, lacking in nothing." James focused on the present— suffering matures and conforms Christians more to Christ's likeness in this life. Peter focused on the future: suffering enhances the believer's ability to function in glory.

9

III. CHRISTIANS ARE BROUGHT TO GLORY THROUGH
SUFFERING

A. 2 Corinthians 4:17—Our "momentary, light affliction is
producing for us an eternal weight of glory far beyond
all comparison." Whereas suffering does make us stron-
ger now—it helps us to endure with patience, increases
our faith, teaches us to trust God, and leads us to depend
on Christ and His Word—it also affects how we will
function later. That's why Paul went on to say our focus
isn't on the now but on the future: "We look not at the
things which are seen, but at the things which are not
seen; for the things which are seen are temporal, but the
things which are not seen are eternal" (v. 18).

B. 2 Timothy 2:12—"If we endure, we shall also reign with
Him." The greater our endurance through suffering, the
greater our eternal reward, which primarily is the ability
to glorify God.

IV. CHRISTIANS ARE IDENTIFIED WITH CHRIST IN THEIR
SUFFERING

Christians are identified with their Master because, like Him,
they suffer to enter their glory.

A. Luke 24:25-26—Christ said to the disciples on the road to
Emmaus, "O foolish men and slow of heart to believe in
all that the prophets have spoken! Was it not necessary
for the Christ to suffer these things and to enter into His
glory?" Our Lord had to explain that His future glory
required that He suffer. We're to expect the same.

B. Hebrews 2:10—"It was fitting for Him, for whom are all
things, and through whom are all things, in bringing
many sons to glory, to perfect the author of their salvation through sufferings." Jesus was the author of our
salvation, bringing us to glory through His suffering.

C. Hebrews 5:8-9—"Although [Jesus] was a Son, He learned
obedience from the things which He suffered; and having

10

been made perfect, He became to all who obey Him the
source of eternal salvation."

D. Matthew 10:21-24—Our Lord warned, "Brother will
deliver up brother to death, and a father his child; and
children will rise up against parents, and cause them to
be put to death. And you will be hated by all on account of My name, but it is the one who has endured
to the end who will be saved. . . . A disciple is not above
his teacher, nor a slave above his master." A disciple is
like his teacher and a slave like his master. Since Jesus
suffered, all His disciples can expect to suffer also (cf.
John 13:16).

Conclusion

The path to glory for Christ was the path of unjust suffering.
That's our path also. Our Lord endured suffering with perfect
patience and was exalted to the highest point of glory. He is
our example of how to respond to suffering.

Focusing on the Facts

1. What is the theme of 1 Peter 2:21-25 (see p. 7)?
2. What two categories of truth does 1 Peter emphasize (see
   p. 8)?
3. First Peter clearly shows that those most blessed in the faith
   _____ the most (see p. 8).
4. What did John and James say about loving the world? How
   will that affect a Christian's attitude toward the society in
   which he or she lives (1 John 2:15; James 4:4; see p. 8)?
5. Why shouldn't the fact that Christians are called to suffer be
   surprising to us (see p. 9)?
6. Suffering is God's way of _____ His people spiritually
   (see p. 9).
7. In what way will suffering be useful to us throughout
   eternity (see p. 9)?

8. How does suffering identify a Christian with his or her Master (see p. 10)?

9. Our Lord is our _____ of how to respond to suffering (see p. 11).

Pondering the Principles

1. Often we see suffering in the world and philosophically shrug it off as a condition of living—there seems to be nothing special about suffering because so many people, both good and bad, suffer. But the Puritan John Arrowsmith wrote, "There is as much difference between the sufferings of the saints and those of the ungodly as there is between the cords with which the executioner pinions a condemned malefactor and the bandages wherewith a tender surgeon binds his patient" (cited in *The Golden Treasury of Puritan Quotations,* edited by I. D. E. Thomas [Edinburgh: Banner of Truth Trust, 1977], p. 289). Do you see your own suffering as God's special dealing with you to bring you into greater glory?

2. We often regard suffering as if it's to be avoided at all costs, yet it's often the best display of a life transformed by Christ. Robert Murray McCheyne, a Scottish minister of the previous century, said, "There is a great want about all Christians who have not suffered. Some flowers must be broken or bruised before they emit any fragrance" (cited in *More Gathered Gold: A Treasury of Quotations for Christians,* edited by John Blanchard [Welwyn, Eng.: Evangelical Press, 1986], p. 315). Do you view afflictions, trials, and sufferings as things to be avoided, or as the greatest opportunities to project the fragrance of a transformed life?

2

The Suffering Jesus:
An Example for Every Christian

Outline

Introduction

Review

Lesson
I. Christ Is Our Example (vv. 21b-23)
    A. We're to Follow His Pattern (v. 21b)
    B. We're to Follow His Reactions (vv. 22-23)
        1. He committed no sin in word or deed
        2. He didn't strike back
        3. He didn't make threats
        4. He entrusted Himself to God

Conclusion

Introduction

First Peter 2:21-25 says, "You have been called for this purpose,
since Christ also suffered for you, leaving you an example for
you to follow in His steps, who committed no sin, nor was any
deceit found in His mouth; and while being reviled, He did not
revile in return; while suffering, He uttered no threats, but kept
entrusting Himself to Him who judges righteously; and He
Himself bore our sins in His body on the cross, that we might
die to sin and live to righteousness; for by His wounds you

13

were healed. For you were continually straying like sheep, but now you have returned to the Shepherd and Guardian of your souls."

The name *Jesus Christ* evokes many images in the minds of people. Some picture Him as a baby in a manger—the Christ of Christmas. Others picture Him as a child, perhaps living in the home of a carpenter or confounding the religious leaders of Jerusalem. Many picture Him as a compassionate and powerful healer who healed the sick and raised the dead. Still others picture a bold and fiery preacher speaking the Word of God to great crowds. And there are those who see Him as the consummate man—a model of goodness, kindness, sympathy, concern, care, tenderness, forgiveness, wisdom, understanding, and trust in God.

Yet the one image of Christ that surpasses all the rest is Jesus Christ on the cross. The apostle Paul said to the Corinthians, "I determined to know nothing among you except Jesus Christ, and Him crucified" (1 Cor. 2:2). To know Christ crucified is to know Him as the author and finisher of your faith—the truest picture of His Person and work.

Christ's suffering on the cross is the focal point of the Christian faith. That's where the deity, humanity, work, and suffering of Christ is most clearly seen. First Peter 2:21-25 shows that the suffering of Jesus had three great effects: it allowed Him to serve as our example, substitute, and shepherd.

Review

According to the previous verse, Christians have been called to suffer with patient endurance (see pp. 8-9). Because we are at odds with the world, we will suffer persecution at various times and in various ways. That pleases God because He knows it will mature us and perfect our ability to glorify Him in heaven (see pp. 9-10). Beyond those realities, such suffering identifies us with our Lord Jesus Christ, for we suffer as He suffered (see pp. 10-11).

Lesson

I. CHRIST IS OUR EXAMPLE (vv. 21b-23)

"Christ . . . suffered for you, leaving you an example for you to follow in His steps, who committed no sin, nor was any deceit found in His mouth; and while being reviled, He did not revile in return; while suffering, He uttered no threats, but kept entrusting Himself to Him who judges righteously."

The suffering of Christ sets the standard for the suffering of Christians. The greater our suffering for righteousness in this life, the greater our glory in the life to come.

Jesus was executed as a criminal on a cross. Yet He was guilty of no crime—no wrong, no trespass, no sin. He never had an evil thought or spoke an evil word. His was the most unjust execution ever inflicted on a human being. Yet it shows us that though a person may be perfectly within the will of God—greatly loved and gifted, perfectly righteous and obedient—he may still experience unjust suffering. Like Jesus we may be misunderstood, misrepresented, hated, persecuted, and even murdered.

Are Suffering Christians Out of God's Will?

Some contemporary false teachers say that Christians who suffer are out of God's will. Such teaching reflects a shallow and ungodly interpretation of the Bible. Scripture clearly states that Christians will suffer for their faith (Matt. 5:11-12; 10:17; 24:9; Luke 21:12; John 15:20; 16:2; 2 Tim. 3:12). To say that believers who are suffering for their faith aren't "claiming their resources" is heresy. Jesus Christ was perfectly in the will of God— perfectly righteous, gifted, and loved by God—yet suffered unjustly on a cross. Those who suffer for their faith in Christ are like their Master and perfectly within God's will.

15

A. We're to Follow His Pattern (v. 21*b*)

"Christ . . . suffered for you, leaving you an example for you to follow in His steps."

The Greek word translated "example" (*hupogrammos*) refers to a pattern that is placed under a piece of paper to be traced. Like children who learn their letters by using tracing paper over a pattern, we are to trace our lives according to the pattern Jesus Christ has laid down for us.

We follow His pattern by walking "in His steps." "Steps" translates the Greek word *ichnos*, which refers to a track, or line of footprints. We are to walk in Christ's footprints because His was a righteous walk. It was also a walk of unjust suffering, which is part of the walk of righteousness. Some suffer more than others, but all who follow after Christ experience some suffering.

B. We're to Follow His Reactions (vv. 22-23)

"[Christ] committed no sin, nor was any deceit found in His mouth; and while being reviled, He did not revile in return; while suffering, He uttered no threats, but kept entrusting Himself to Him who judges righteously."

Peter wanted his readers to look closely at the suffering of Christ. The cross was the time of maximum suffering for our Lord and would have been prominent in Peter's mind because he personally witnessed his Lord's pain—though from afar. So verses 22-23 take us to the cross, explaining in the process the meaning of Isaiah 53—the clearest Old Testament chapter on the suffering of the Messiah.

1. He committed no sin in word or deed

   Isaiah 53:9 says, "He [the Messiah] had done no violence." "Violence" is translated "lawlessness" in the Septuagint, the Greek version of the Hebrew Old Testament. The translators understood that the violence spoken of in Isaiah 53:9 is violence against God's law—or sin, which "is lawlessness" (1 John 3:4).

Peter, under the inspiration of the Holy Spirit, understood the violence spoken of in Isaiah 53:9 in the same way. Thus 1 Peter 2:22 is saying that in spite of the unjust treatment Christ had to endure, He committed no sin. Christ was impeccable—He did not and could not sin (cf. 1 Pet. 1:19).

Isaiah 53:9 adds, "Nor was there any deceit in His mouth." That strengthens the idea that Jesus committed no sin because sin usually makes its first appearance in what we say. The Hebrew word translated "deceit" refers to any sin of the tongue, such as deception, innuendo, or slander.

James 3:2 says, "If anyone does not stumble in what he says, he is a perfect man." That's because only someone who is perfect can avoid sinning with his mouth, for what we say is but a reflection of what's in our heart (Mark 7:21). In Jesus there was no sin, either externally or internally.

a) Luke 23:41—One of the thieves crucified with Jesus said to the other, "We indeed [suffer] justly, for we are receiving what we deserve for our deeds; but this man [Jesus] has done nothing wrong."

b) John 8:46—Jesus said, "Which one of you convicts Me of sin?" No one could truthfully accuse Jesus of sin.

c) 2 Corinthians 5:21—Paul said of God's working in Christ, "He made Him who knew no sin to be sin on our behalf."

d) Hebrews 4:15—Jesus "has been tempted in all things as we are, yet without sin."

e) Hebrews 7:26—Jesus, our High Priest, is "holy, innocent, undefiled, separated from sinners and exalted above the heavens."

f) 1 Peter 3:18—"Christ . . . died for sins once for all, the just for the unjust."

g) 1 John 3:5—"In [Jesus Christ] there is no sin."

In all the circumstances of His ministry on earth our Lord was absolutely sinless. He was the most unjustly treated person who ever lived on earth because, unlike you and me, He never did anything wrong. He is the perfect model of how we are to respond to unjust treatment because He endured far worse treatment than any person who will ever live, yet He never sinned.

2. He didn't strike back

Isaiah 53:7 says of the Messiah, "He was oppressed and He was afflicted, yet He did not open His mouth; like a lamb that is led to slaughter, and like a sheep that is silent before its shearers, so He did not open His mouth." That reflects the attitude of Jesus before His tormentors: "While being reviled, He did not revile in return" (1 Pet. 2:23). Though under sustained provocation, Jesus spoke no evil because there was no sin in His heart.

However, under similar provocation our reaction would probably be more like that of the apostle Paul's. When Paul was on trial before the Sanhedrin, the high priest Ananias ordered him struck on the mouth. Paul's immediate response to Ananias was, "God is going to strike you, you whitewashed wall!" (Acts 23:3). Paul immediately had to apologize—such an exclamation was against the law (vv. 4-5; cf. Ex. 22:28). Paul wasn't perfect, and he's not the standard of righteousness. Only Christ is a perfect standard of how to handle the reviling of one's enemies.

The Greek word translated "reviled" pictures the continuous piling up of one abuse on top of another. Jesus was consistent in His response to such treatment: He was silent (cf. Matt. 26:57-68; 27:11-14; Mark 14:53-65; 15:1-5; Luke 23:8-9). Christians, like their Master, are never to abuse those who abuse them.

3. He didn't make threats

Jesus "uttered no threats" in the face of incredible suffering (1 Pet. 2:23). He was spit on, His beard was pulled out, a crown of thorns was crushed onto His head, and nails were driven through His flesh to pin Him to a cross. In any other person such unjust treatment would have caused feelings of retaliation to well up and burst out, but not in Christ. He was the Son of God—creator and sustainer of the universe, holy, sinless, and with the power to send His tormentors into eternal flames. Yet instead of threatening them He said, "Father, forgive them; for they do not know what they are doing" (Luke 23:34). Christ died for sinners, including those who persecuted Him. He knew the glory of salvation could be reached only through the path of suffering, so He accepted His suffering without bitterness, anger, or a spirit of retaliation.

4. He entrusted Himself to God

First Peter 3:9 says Christians are not to be "returning evil for evil, or insult for insult, but giving a blessing instead." That was Jesus' attitude. He was able to do that because He "kept entrusting Himself to Him who judges righteously" (1 Pet. 2:23). The word translated "entrusting" (Gk., *paradidōmi*) means "to hand over for someone to keep." In every instance of suffering our Lord handed over the circumstance and Himself to God. The word "Himself," though not found in the Greek text of 1 Peter, accurately reflects the full meaning of the text.

Christ's last words on the cross show His trust in God: "Father, into Thy hands I commit My spirit" (Luke 23:46). Our Lord was confident in the righteous judgment of God and the glory that would be His. That allowed Him to calmly accept tremendous suffering. That's the way we're to respond when confronted with unjust persecution on the job or in our families or other relationships. When we retaliate we forfeit the blessing and reward that suffering is meant to bring. It shows we lack the confidence we ought to have in

19

God's ability to make things right in His own time, which will include punishing the unjust and rewarding those who are faithful in suffering.

Bible commentator Alan Stibbs wrote, "In . . . the unique instance of our Lord's passion, when the sinless One suffered as if He were the worst of sinners, and bore the extreme penalty of sin, there is a double sense in which He may have acknowledged God as the righteous Judge. On the one hand, because voluntarily, and in fulfillment of God's will, He was taking the sinner's place and bearing sin, He did not protest at what He had to suffer. Rather He consciously recognized that it was the penalty righteously due to sin. So He handed Himself over to be punished. He recognized that in letting such shame, pain and curse fall upon Him, the righteous God was judging righteously. On the other hand, because He Himself was sinless, He also believed that in due time God, as the righteous Judge, would vindicate Him as righteous, and exalt Him from the grave, and reward Him for what He had willingly endured for others' sake by giving Him the right completely to save them from the penalty and power of their own wrongdoing" (*The First Epistle of Peter* [Grand Rapids: Eerdmans, 1971], p. 119). When we entrust ourselves to God as the righteous Judge, we are following Christ's example by looking to God for vindication, exaltation, and reward.

Conclusion

I believe that in days to come Christians will become increasingly unpopular with secular society. Strong stands for the truth of Scripture and the gospel message may soon become intolerable. That will result in unjust treatment of Christians.

The prospect of such treatment ought to drive us to passages such as 1 Peter 2:21-25 for reassurance. Here we learn that like our Lord, we are to walk the path of suffering to attain the glory of reward and exaltation in the future. That realization surely prompted Stephen to fix his eyes on Jesus in glory and

20

ask God to forgive his murderers (Acts 7:54-60). He entrusted himself to God, knowing that He would vindicate him.

In May of 1555 Bishop Hugh Latimer, soon to be burned at the stake for his anti-papal, Reformed convictions, wrote, "Die once we must; how and where, we know not. . . . Here is not our home; let us therefore accordingly consider things, having always before our eyes that heavenly Jerusalem, and the way thereto in persecution" (Harold S. Darby, *Hugh Latimer* [London: The Epworth Press, 1953], p. 237). Later that year both Latimer and his friend Ridley were fed to the flames, but not until Latimer—astonishingly composed—said to his colleague, "Be of good comfort, master Ridley, and play the man. We shall this day light such a candle, by God's grace, in England, as I trust shall never be put out" (p. 247). In no way did Jesus leave His "example" (1 Pet. 2:21) in vain!

Focusing on the Facts

1. What single image of Christ surpasses all the rest as the truest picture of His Person and work (see p. 14)?
2. First Peter 2:21-25 shows that Christ is our _____, _____, and _____ (see p. 14).
3. The greater our _____ for righteousness in this life, the greater our _____ in the life to come (see p. 15).
4. The suffering of Christ shows us that though a person may be perfectly within the will of God, what still might happen (see p. 15)?
5. Show from Scripture that those who suffer for their faith in Christ are like their Master and perfectly within God's will (see p. 15).
6. How does the Greek word translated "example" picture the believer's relationship to Christ (1 Pet. 2:21; see p. 16)?
7. Why are Christians to walk in the footprints of Christ (see p. 16)?
8. What Old Testament chapter does 1 Peter 2:22-23 explain (see p. 16)?
9. In 1 Peter 2:22 Peter says that in spite of the unjust treatment Christ had to endure, He committed _____ _____ (see p. 17).

10. James 3:2 says, "If anyone does not stumble in what he says, he is a perfect man." Why is that true? How does that truth reflect on Jesus Christ (see p. 17)?
11. Why is Jesus the perfect model of how we are to respond to unjust treatment (see p. 18)?
12. How does Isaiah 53:7 reflect the attitude of Jesus before His tormentors (see p. 18)?
13. Compare how Jesus and Paul responded to similar unjust suffering. Whose response would we more likely emulate (see p. 18)?
14. Christians, like their Master, are never to _____ those who _____ them (see p. 18).
15. Describe the extent of Christ's trust in God (see p. 19).
16. When we retaliate what do we forfeit (see p. 19)?
17. What prompted Stephen to ask God to forgive his murderers (Acts 7:54-60; see pp. 20-21)?

Pondering the Principles

1. Jesus suffered unimaginable humiliation. During His trial those present "spat in His face and beat Him with their fists; and others slapped Him, and said, 'Prophesy to us, You Christ; who is the one who hit You?'" (Matt. 26:67-68). One commentator noted, "The mockers received no reply to this question. Jesus was silent. But we may give a different turn to the inquiry, and the answer will prove consolatory. Let those who are earnestly seeking salvation, and the contrite in heart, humbly inquire, 'Who it was that smote the Lord?' and they will receive a satisfactory reply. At first, indeed, it will alarm them; for it will be, 'not those miscreants; but it is thou who hast made Me to suffer with thy sins, and wearied Me with thy iniquities. For thy transgressions was I smitten.' And when He Himself prophesies this to you by His Spirit—how evident it will then become to you; how will you humble yourselves in the dust before Him; how the wish will then depart to lay the blame upon Caiaphas, Annas, and the spearmen; how vitally are you persuaded that they were only your representatives, and how will you hang down your heads, and learn to smite upon your breasts with the publican! How will you tremble for your souls, and earnestly seek for salvation and a Mediator!" (F. W. Krummacher, *The Suffering Savior* [Chicago: Moody,

1947], p. 184). Whereas the example of Christ's suffering ought to hearten us in times of persecution, perhaps even more it ought make us grateful for His willingness to suffer for us sinners (cf. Rom. 5:8). Take time now to express your gratitude to our Lord for His willingness to suffer on our behalf.

2. Your speech indicates the state of your heart—whether evil or grace dominates it. A. W. Tozer has written, "The fear that keeps us quiet when faith and love and loyalty cry out for us to speak is surely evil and must be judged as evil before the bar of eternal justice" (cited in *Signposts: A Collection of Sayings from A. W. Tozer*, edited by Harry Verploegh [Wheaton, Ill.: Victor Books, 1988], p. 195). Jesus' speech in His time of trial showed a heart filled with the grace of God—He spoke no evil but answered with the truth. Does your speech show the grace of God even when you are facing a severe trial?

3

The Suffering Jesus:
Our Substitute and Shepherd

Outline

Introduction

Review
I. Christ Is Our Example (vv. 21b-23)

Lesson
II. Christ Is Our Substitute (v. 24)
A. The Meaning of His Sin Bearing
B. The Extent of His Sin Bearing
C. The Means of His Sin Bearing
D. The Reason for His Sin Bearing
E. The Punishment for His Sin Bearing
III. Christ Is Our Shepherd (v. 25)
A. The Turning
B. The Title
C. The Task

Introduction

First Peter 2:21-25 says, "You have been called for this purpose,
since Christ also suffered for you, leaving you an example for
you to follow in His steps, who committed no sin, nor was any
deceit found in His mouth; and while being reviled, He did not
revile in return; while suffering, He uttered no threats, but kept

entrusting Himself to Him who judges righteously; and He Himself bore our sins in His body on the cross, that we might die to sin and live to righteousness; for by His wounds you were healed. For you were continually straying like sheep, but now you have returned to the Shepherd and Guardian of your souls."

Those verses have much to say about the kind of life that will most effectively manifest Christ to an ungodly culture. As believers we are called to a submissive role in society, just as our Lord was.

Review

I.   CHRIST IS OUR EXAMPLE (vv. 21b-23; pp. 15-21)

Lesson

II. CHRIST IS OUR SUBSTITUTE (v. 24)

"He Himself bore our sins in His body on the cross, that we might die to sin and live to righteousness; for by His wounds you were healed."

Peter was saying that Christ suffered on our behalf, alluding to Isaiah's description of the substitutionary, sin-bearing death of the Messiah (Isa. 53:4-5, 11). The substitutionary death of Christ is an essential truth of the Christian faith.

Commentator Leon Morris wrote, "Redemption is substitutionary, for it means that Christ paid the price that we could not pay, paid it in our stead, and we go free. Justification interprets our salvation judicially, and as the New Testament sees it Christ took our legal liability, took it in our stead. Reconciliation means the making of people to be at one by the taking away of the cause of hostility. In this case the cause is sin, and Christ removed that cause for us. We could not deal with sin. He could and did, and did it in such a way that it is reckoned to us. Propitiation points us to the removal of the divine wrath, and Christ has done this by bearing the wrath for us. It was our sin which drew it down; it was He who bore it. . . . Was there a price to be paid? He paid it. Was there a victory to be won? He won it. Was there a penalty to be borne? He bore it. Was there a judgment to be faced? He faced it" (*The Cross in the New Testament* [Grand Rapids: Eerdmans, 1965], p. 405). Redemption, justification, reconciliation, removal of sin, and propitiation are all corollaries of the substitutionary work of Christ on the cross.

The apostle Paul also emphasized the substitutionary work of Christ. He said that God "made Him who knew no sin to be sin on our behalf, that we might become the righteousness of God in Him" (2 Cor. 5:21)—that "Christ redeemed us from the curse of the Law, having become a curse for us" (Gal. 3:13). "To put it bluntly and plainly," says Morris, "if Christ is not my Substitute, I still occupy the place of a condemned sinner. If my sins and my guilt are not transferred to Him, if He did not take them upon Himself, then surely they remain with me. If He did not deal with my sins, I must face their consequences. If my penalty was not borne by Him, it still hangs over me" (p. 410).

Was Christ's Suffering Unfair?

Some say it's immoral to teach that God would take on human flesh and bear the sins of men and women in their stead. They say it's unfair to transfer the penalty of sin from a guilty person to an innocent person. But that's not what happened on the cross.

Morris explains, "In the process of salvation God is not transferring penalty from one man (guilty) to another man (innocent). He is bearing it Himself. The absolute oneness between the Father and the Son in the work of the atonement must not for a moment be lost sight of. When Christ substitutes for sinful man in His death that is God Himself bearing the consequences of our sin, God saving man at cost to Himself, not at cost to someone else. As Leonard Hodgson puts it, 'He wills that sin shall be punished, but He does not will that sin shall be punished without also willing that the punishment shall fall on Himself.' In part the atonement is to be understood as a process

27

whereby God absorbs in Himself the consequences of man's sin" (p. 410).

On the cross Christ willingly took on our sin and bore its penalty. Nothing was pushed on Him. If He had not willed to take our sin and accept its punishment, as sinners we would have borne the punishment of sin in hell forever. Christ's work on the cross wasn't unfair—it was God's love in action!

First Peter 2:24 says that Christ "Himself bore our sins." The Greek word translated "Himself" is emphatic—it was Christ *Himself* who took on sin and bore its penalty. He bore it willingly and voluntarily—and He bore it alone. He indeed was "the Lamb of God who takes away the sin of the world" (John 1:29).

Jesus Christ Superstar?

Some think Jesus died as a martyr—that He is a great example of someone dying for a cause. That's the "Jesus Christ Superstar" mentality. It pictures Jesus as someone so committed to a cause that He was willing to die for it. But whereas a martyr can be a great example of suffering, he can't be a substitute or remove sin. Only God could do that, and that's exactly what Jesus did.

A. The Meaning of His Sin Bearing

First Peter 3:18 speaks of the substitutionary death of Christ: "Christ . . . died for sins once for all, the just for the unjust." When Peter said He "bore" our sins (1 Pet. 2:24), he used a term that means "to carry a massive, heavy weight." That's what sin is. It's so heavy that Romans 8:22 says, "The whole creation groans and suffers" under its weight. Only Jesus could remove such a weight from us.

The express idea of Christ's bearing our sins is stated only in 1 Peter 2:24 and Hebrews 9:28. The concept is more frequently declared in the Old Testament.

1. Numbers 14:33-34—God said to Israel, "Your sons shall be shepherds for forty years in the wilderness, and they shall suffer for your unfaithfulness, until your corpses lie in the wilderness. According to the number of days which you spied out the land, forty days, for every day you shall bear your guilt a year, even forty years, and you shall know My opposition." When God brought Israel out of Egypt and led them to Kadesh Barnea, Israel sent spies into Canaan. But even though God had promised Canaan to Israel, most of the spies brought back a report that dissuaded Israel from entering the Promised Land (Num. 13). When God said Israel would bear its guilt (Num. 14:34), He meant the people would bear the punishment of their sin of rejecting God and failing to trust Him (cf. Num. 14:11).

2. Ezekiel 18:20—"The soul that sinneth, it shall die. The son shall not bear the iniquity of the father, neither shall the father bear the iniquity of the son" (KJV*). To "bear the iniquity" means to be punished. In this case the punishment was death.

3. Numbers 18:1—"The Lord said to Aaron, 'You and your sons and your father's household with you shall bear the guilt in connection with the sanctuary; and you and your sons with you shall bear the guilt in connection with your priesthood'" (cf. 18:23).

4. Ezekiel 4:4—God gave Israel a symbolic demonstration of sin's punishment by telling Ezekiel, "Lie down on your left side, and lay the iniquity of the house of Israel on it; you shall bear their iniquity for the number of days that you lie on it" (cf. 44:10-12).

When Peter said that Christ "bore our sins" (v. 24), he meant that Christ bore the penalty for our sins. He endured physical and spiritual death. When Jesus cried out on the cross, "My God, My God, why hast Thou forsaken Me?"

---

*King James Version.

(Matt. 27:46), His was the cry of spiritual death. That was the penalty for bearing our sins.

B. The Extent of His Sin Bearing

Christ bore the sin of all sinners.

1. John 3:16—"God so loved the world, that He gave His only begotten Son, that whoever believes in Him should not perish, but have eternal life." The atoning work of Christ was as extensive as the love of God toward the world: it embraced all.

2. 2 Corinthians 5:19—In Christ's sacrificial death "God was in Christ reconciling the world to Himself." Many think that Christ bore the sins and punishment only of the elect. But I believe that God loved the whole world and therefore provided a sacrifice as great as His love.

3. 1 Timothy 2:6—Christ "gave Himself as a ransom for all."

4. 1 Timothy 4:10—God in Christ "is the Savior of all men, especially of believers." Christ has shown Himself to be the Savior of all men, but that becomes a spiritual reality for believers only. God gave a gift to the world by paying the penalty of sin, but only those who believe receive that gift (John 1:12).

5. Titus 2:11—"The grace of God has appeared, bringing salvation to all men."

6. Hebrews 2:9—"We do see Him who has been made for a little while lower than the angels, namely, Jesus, because of the suffering of death crowned with glory and honor, that by the grace of God He might taste death for everyone."

7. 1 John 2:2—Christ "is the propitiation for our sins; and not for ours only, but also for those of the whole world."

8. 1 John 4:9—"The love of God was manifested in us, that God has sent His only begotten Son into the

world so that we might live through Him. In this is love, not that we loved God, but that He loved us and sent His Son to be the propitiation for our sins." The word *our* embodies an extensive provision—one that provides a sufficient sacrifice for the sins of all men but is only applied to those who believe.

Our Hope Rests Here

British preacher Charles Haddon Spurgeon loved the doctrine of substitution. Here are assorted nuggets taken from his preaching on this precious topic (cited from Tom Carter's *Spurgeon at His Best* [Grand Rapids: Baker, 1988], pp. 200-201):

- "In one word, the great fact on which the Christian's hope rests is *substitution*. The vicarious sacrifice of Christ for the sinner, Christ's suffering for the sinner, Christ's being made sin for us that we might be made the righteousness of God in him, Christ offering up a true and proper substitutionary sacrifice in the place of as many as the Father gave him, who are recognized by their trusting in him—this is the cardinal fact of the gospel."

- "There is no doctrine that fires my soul with such delight as that of substitution."

- "Substitution is the very marrow of the whole Bible, the soul of salvation, the essence of the gospel. We ought to saturate all our sermons with it, for it is the lifeblood of a gospel ministry."

- "I am incapable of moving one inch away from the old faith. One thing I know—the gospel of substitution. And one thing I do—preach it."

- "If you put away the doctrine of the substitutionary sacrifice of Christ, you have disembowelled the gospel, and torn from it its very heart."

- "I pray God that every stone of this [church] may tumble to its ruin and every timber be shivered to atoms, before there should stand on this platform a man to preach who denies

C. The Means of His Sin Bearing

Jesus bore our sins "in His body on the cross [lit., "wood"]" (1 Pet. 2:24). It was God's plan that Christ be lifted up to die (cf. John 12:32-33). Paul says that Christ had to be hung on a tree to fulfill the prediction of becoming a curse for us (Gal. 3:13; cf. Deut. 21:23). Jesus bore our sins by enduring the wrath of God as He hung on a cross of wood.

D. The Reason for His Sin Bearing

The purpose for Jesus' substitutionary sacrifice was that "we might die to sin and live to righteousness" (1 Pet. 2:24). The text doesn't say Christ died so we could go to heaven, have peace, or experience love. Christ died to bring about a transformation: to make saints out of sinners.

The Greek word translated "die" (apoginomai) is used only here in the New Testament. It means "to be away from, depart, be missing, or cease existing." The Greek particle apo is used in classical Greek with reference to the dead as the "dearly departed." Christ's substitutionary work causes a person to depart from sin and enter into a new life pattern: a life of righteousness.

The apostle Paul said, "Our old self was crucified with [Christ], that our body of sin might be done away with, that we should no longer be slaves to sin" (Rom. 6:6). Our identification with Christ in His death results in our walking "in newness of life" (v. 4). We have died to sin; thus it no longer has a claim on us. First Peter 2:24 echoes that thought: our identification with Christ in His death is a departure from sin and a new direction in life (see John MacArthur, Freedom from Sin: The Believer's Ongoing Battle [Panorama City, Calif.: The Master's Communication, 1989]).

E. The Punishment for His Sin Bearing

Peter's statement "by His wounds you are healed" is an allusion to Isaiah 53:5. The Greek word translated "wounds" (*mōlōps*) refers to the scars, bruises, and welts from a whipping. The punishment Jesus bore in His body—the scourging, mockery, and crucifixion—became a means for our spiritual healing. Both Peter and Isaiah were not referring to physical but spiritual healing in their references to the suffering of Christ.

Physical Healing in the Atonement?

There is a sense in which physical healing took place in the atoning work of Christ. But that healing waits to be realized in the future. The healing of the atonement will bring about our resurrection in glory, where there will be no pain or suffering (Rev. 21:1-4; 22:1-3).

Matthew 8:16 says of Jesus' healing ministry, "When evening had come, they brought to Him many who were demon-possessed; and He cast out the spirits with a word, and healed all who were ill in order that what was spoken through Isaiah the prophet might be fulfilled, saying, 'He Himself took our infirmities, and carried away our diseases.' " Some say that means we're to claim healing in the atonement, and in a sense that is correct. Jesus healed people to illustrate the healing in the glory to come. But that's not yet realized. If the healing of the atonement were fully realized now, no Christian would ever be sick or die. The atoning work of Christ spiritually transforms us now and will physically transform us in the future.

III. CHRIST IS OUR SHEPHERD (v. 25)

"You were continually straying like sheep, but now you have returned to the Shepherd and Guardian of your souls."

Here Peter was alluding to Isaiah 53:6: "All of us like sheep have gone astray, each of us has turned to his own way; but the Lord has caused the iniquity of us all to fall on Him." If the Lord had not provided a sacrifice for sin, He could never have brought us into His fold.

33

A. The Turning

The Greek word translated "returned" refers to repentance—a turning from one thing toward another. It's what the prodigal son did when he turned from his sin to his father (Luke 15:11-32). The believer turns to a Person—Jesus Christ—not just a system of theology or religion. Believers have turned over their whole lives to their Shepherd and Guardian.

B. The Title

Jesus referred to Himself as the "good shepherd" (John 10:11, 14). First Peter 5:4 refers to Him as the "Chief Shepherd." Those are significant titles because the Old Testament affirms that "the Lord is my shepherd" (Ps. 23:1; italics added; cf. Ezek. 34:23-24; 37:24). In 1 Peter 2:25 Peter implicitly affirms the deity of Christ.

C. The Task

The task of a shepherd is to guard sheep. The Greek word translated "shepherd" (*poimen*) can also be translated "pastor," whereas the word translated "guardian" (*episkopos*) is also translated "bishop" or "overseer." Both terms describe the responsibilities of elders (e.g., 1 Pet. 5:2). Jesus guards, oversees, leads, and supervises His flock. He said that "the good shepherd lays down His life for the sheep" (John 10:11). That's exactly what He did to bring us to Himself.

Conclusion

Jesus suffered greatly as our example, substitute, and shepherd. Spurgeon said, "When the pangs shoot through our body, and ghastly death appears in view, people see the patience of the dying Christian. *Our infirmities become the black velvet on which the diamond of God's love glitters all the more brightly.* Thank God I can suffer! Thank God I can be made the object of shame and contempt, for in this way God shall be glorified" (*Spurgeon at His Best*, p. 202; italics added). That's a good summation of Peter's point: If you're a Christian, expect to suffer.

34

Because we believers are aliens and strangers in the world, waging war against fleshly lusts and being slandered and persecuted, we must expect to suffer in the name of the One who endured all manner of suffering for us (1 Pet. 2:21-25). The central thrust of Peter's message is to remind us of the necessity of suffering. When in the midst of suffering we sin in thought, word, or deed by retaliating, we lose our victory and damage our testimony.

Revelation 12:11 says that the brethren "overcame [Satan] because of the blood of the Lamb and because of the word of their testimony, and they did not love their life even to death." Believers overcome the insults, persecutions, and accusations of Satan by the blood of the Lamb. That's the power of God. They're overcomers because their testimony is not lost by retaliation during times of persecution, and because they won't compromise even to the point of death. They are willing to suffer. If we have those kinds of attitudes we will overcome too.

Focusing on the Facts

1. Like our Lord, as believers we are called to a _____ role in society (see p. 26).
2. What passage of the Old Testament did Peter allude to in 1 Peter 2:24? What does that passage say about the Messiah (see p. 26)?
3. According to Leon Morris, what does the word *propitiation* points us to (see pp. 26-27)?
4. What did God do in the process of salvation concerning the penalty for sin (see p. 27)?
5. Christ's work on the cross wasn't _____—it was _____ in action (see p. 27).
6. What's wrong with the idea that Jesus is just a great example of someone who died for a cause (see p. 28)?
7. What Old Testament passages explain the meaning of bearing sin? What exactly was borne when Christ bore our sins (see pp. 28-29)?
8. Christ bore the sin of _____ sinners (see p. 30).
9. What is the great fact on which the Christian's hope rests (see p. 31)?
10. How specifically did Jesus bear our sins (see p. 32)?

11. Christ died to bring about a _____ (see p. 32).
12. According to 1 Peter 2:24, what does identification with Christ in His death represent (see p. 32)?
13. What are the scourging, mockery, and crucifixion of Christ a means of for believers (see p. 33)?
14. In what sense did physical healing take place in the atoning work of Christ (see p. 33)?
15. By naming Christ as the shepherd of believers, what was Peter implying (1 Pet. 2:25; see p. 34)?

Pondering the Principles

1. We are often prone to be more troubled about a great affliction we must suffer than "trivial" sins we commit. Yet in God's economy, "There is more evil in a drop of sin than in a sea of affliction" (Thomas Watson as cited in *More Gathered Gold,* John Blanchard, ed. [Welwyn, Eng.: Evangelical Press, 1986], p. 325). Jesus determined to see sinners cleansed from sin rather than escape the affliction of the cross and the outpouring of God's wrath. Are you concerned more about your personal comfort or avoiding sin?

2. We studiously avoid suffering, and surely we are not called to endure unnecessary suffering. Yet at times our faith demands the endurance of trials. Our Great Shepherd was faced with that necessity to save His sheep, and He walked into suffering with open eyes. British pastor and missionary Oswald Chambers wrote, "He deliberately laid down His life without any possibility of deliverance. There was no compulsion, it was a sacrifice made with a free mind; nor was there anything . . . impulsive about it, He laid down His life with a clear knowledge of what He was doing. Jesus understood what was coming, it was not a foreboding, but a certainty; not a catastrophe which might happen, but an ordained certainty in the decrees of God, and He knew it" (cited in *Oswald Chambers: The Best from All His Books,* vol. 2, Harry Verploegh, ed. [Nashville: Oliver Nelson, 1989], p. 270). In those cases where your faith in Christ demands that you walk the path of suffering, are you willing to walk for Him as He walked for you?

4

The Triumph of Christ's Suffering—
Part 1

Outline

Introduction
A. Our Model of Enduring Suffering
  1. Peter's theme
  2. Peter's readers
B. Our Model of Triumphing Through Suffering

Lesson
I. The Triumph of Bearing the Sins of Humanity (v. 18a)
    A. Christ's Suffering Was Ultimate
    B. Christ's Suffering Was for the Sins of Others
    C. Christ's Suffering Was Unique
    D. Christ's Suffering Was Comprehensive
    E. Christ's Suffering Was Vicarious
    F. Christ's Suffering Was Purposeful

Conclusion

Introduction

A. Our Model of Enduring Suffering

1. Peter's theme

   The theme of 1 Peter is living in the midst of suffering. Throughout the epistle Peter points to Christ as our model of enduring suffering and emphasizes the necessity of suffering in believers' lives.

   a) 1 Peter 2:20-21—"If when you do what is right and suffer for it you patiently endure it, this finds favor with God. For you have been called for this purpose, since Christ also suffered for you, leaving you an example for you to follow in His steps."

   b) 1 Peter 4:1—"Since Christ has suffered in the flesh, arm yourselves also with the same purpose, because he who has suffered in the flesh has ceased from sin."

   c) 1 Peter 4:12-13—"Beloved, do not be surprised at the fiery ordeal among you, which comes upon you for your testing, as though some strange thing were happening to you; but to the degree that you share the sufferings of Christ, keep on rejoicing; so that also at the revelation of His glory, you may rejoice with exultation."

   d) 1 Peter 5:1—"I exhort the elders among you, as your fellow elder and witness of the sufferings of Christ, and a partaker also of the glory that is to be revealed."

2. Peter's readers

   Peter wrote to people who were in the midst of difficult circumstances. Throughout his first letter Peter shows he was aware there were people who desired to harm his readers.

   a) 1 Peter 1:6-7—"You have been distressed by various trials, that the proof of your faith, being more precious than gold which is perishable, even though tested by fire, may be found to result in praise and glory and honor at the revelation of Jesus Christ."

38

b) 1 Peter 2:12—"Keep your behavior excellent among the Gentiles, so that in the thing in which they slander you as evildoers, they may on account of your good deeds . . . glorify God."

c) 1 Peter 3:9—Peter said his readers were not to be "returning evil for evil, or insult for insult, but giving a blessing instead."

d) 1 Peter 3:13—"Who is there to harm you if you prove zealous for what is good?"

e) 1 Peter 4:14—"If you are reviled for the name of Christ, you are blessed, because the Spirit of glory and of God rests upon you."

f) 1 Peter 4:16—"If anyone suffers as a Christian, let him not feel ashamed."

g) 1 Peter 4:19—"Let those also who suffer according to the will of God entrust their souls to a faithful Creator in doing what is right."

h) 1 Peter 5:10—"After you have suffered for a little while, the God of all grace, who called you to His eternal glory in Christ, will Himself perfect, confirm, strengthen and establish you."

When suffering we are to keep our eyes fixed firmly on Christ, "who committed no sin, nor was any deceit found in His mouth; and while being reviled, He did not revile in return; while suffering, He uttered no threats, but kept entrusting Himself to Him who judges righteously" (1 Pet. 2:22-23).

B. Our Model of Triumphing Through Suffering

Christ is also our model of how to triumph through suffering. We aren't simply to maintain a stiff upper lip in the midst of suffering and grit it out. Suffering is to be a time of victory and triumph for us. That's what we see in the life of Christ.

Lesson

First Peter 3:18-22 says, "Christ . . . died for sins once for all, the just for the unjust, in order that He might bring us to God, having been put to death in the flesh, but made alive in the spirit; in which also He went and made proclamation to the spirits now in prison, who once were disobedient, when the patience of God kept waiting in the days of Noah, during the construction of the ark, in which a few, that is, eight persons, were brought safely through the water. And corresponding to that, baptism now saves you—not the removal of dirt from the flesh, but an appeal to God for a good conscience—through the resurrection of Jesus Christ, who is at the right hand of God, having gone into heaven, after angels and authorities and powers had been subjected to Him." The key thought is in verses 18 and 22: though Christ unjustly suffered at the hands of demons and men, He triumphed through the resurrection. Like Him we too will triumph over our unjust suffering.

I. THE TRIUMPH OF BEARING THE SINS OF HUMANITY (v. 18a)

"Christ also died for sins once for all, the just for the unjust, in order that He might bring us to God, having been put to death in the flesh, but made alive in the spirit."

It's an incredible thought that One who was perfectly just would die for the unjust. Pilate was correct when he said of Jesus, "I find no guilt in this man" (Luke 23:4). The charges brought against our Lord were fabricated. The witnesses were bribed, and the conviction itself was illegal.

Yet Christ triumphed through such unjust suffering by bringing us to God. And though believers will never suffer as substitutes or redeemers, God may use their Christlike response to unjust suffering to draw others to Himself.

A. Christ's Suffering Was Ultimate

The word *also* at the beginning of verse 18 points back to believers. We ought not to be surprised that we suffer, because Christ *also* suffered. When the Lord asks us to

40

suffer for His sake, we must realize we are being asked only to endure what He Himself endured for us.

Christ endured suffering to the utmost point: He "died." In contrast, the writer of Hebrews said his readers had not "yet resisted to the point of shedding blood" (Heb. 12:4)—they had not suffered in an ultimate sense by dying for their faith. Some translations of 1 Peter 3:18 say, "Christ suffered" (e.g., KJV) whereas others say that He "died" (e.g., NASB*, NIV**). That's because some Greek manuscripts read one way and some the other. Nevertheless, the meaning behind each term is the same: Christ suffered ultimately in that He died.

B. Christ's Suffering Was for the Sins of Others

Christ died "for sins" (v. 18). When we as believers suffer persecution, criticism, or even death, we are sinners suffering because of the sins of others—whether hatred, anger, envy, or murder. Christ also suffered for sins, but He suffered as the sinless One who bore the sins of the world.

First Peter 2:22 says He "committed no sin." He never thought, said, or did anything evil. Rather, everything He thought, said, and did was perfectly holy. It was the sins of others that placed Him on the cross: of those who shouted, "Crucify Him," those who nailed Him to the cross, and more generally those of the whole world.

Romans 8:3 says that Jesus died "for sin" (cf. Heb. 10:6). He suffered as a sin offering because "the wages of sin is death" (Rom. 6:23). Just as in the Old Testament God required an animal sacrifice to symbolize the need to atone for sin, the New Testament presents Christ as *the* sacrifice who provided not a picture but the reality of atonement for sin.

---

*New American Standard Bible.
**New International Version.

41

C. Christ's Suffering Was Unique

The phrase "once for all" (v. 18) translates the Greek word *hapax*, which means "of perpetual validity, not requiring repetition" (W. E. Vine, *The Expanded Vine's Expository Dictionary of New Testament Words*, John R. Kohlenberger III, ed. [Minneapolis: Bethany, 1984], p. 809). For Jewish people that was a new idea—they had been slaughtering animals for hundreds of years to atone for sin. At Passover as many as a quarter of a million sheep would be slaughtered every year. But Christ's sacrifice was uniquely sufficient for all time.

1. Hebrews 7:26-27—"It was fitting that we should have such a high priest [Jesus Christ], holy, innocent, undefiled, separated from sinners and exalted above the heavens; who does not need daily, like [other] high priests, to offer up sacrifices, first for His own sins, and then for the sins of the people, because this He did once for all when He offered up Himself." The New Covenant in Christ is better than the Old Covenant in Moses because it has a better sacrifice.

2. Hebrews 9:24-28—"Christ did not enter a holy place made with hands, a mere copy of the true one, but into heaven itself, now to appear in the presence of God for us; nor was it that He should offer Himself often, as the high priest enters the holy place year by year with blood not his own. Otherwise, He would have needed to suffer often since the foundation of the world; but now once at the consummation of the ages He has been manifested to put away sin by the sacrifice of Himself. And inasmuch as it is appointed for men to die once and after this comes judgment, so Christ also, having been offered once to bear the sins of many, shall appear a second time for salvation without reference to sin, to those who eagerly await Him."

"It *Is* Finished!"

Unlike any other sacrifice, the atoning death of Christ need never be repeated. Some think Christ must be sacrificed again and again through religious ceremony. That happens in the Roman Catholic mass. But that viewpoint is a direct attack on the unique work of Christ on the cross. You can't sacrifice Christ repeatedly and still affirm with Him, "It is finished!" (John 19:30).

D. Christ's Suffering Was Comprehensive

1. 2 Corinthians 5:14-15—"The love of Christ controls us, having concluded this, that one died for all, therefore all died; and He died for all, that they who live should no longer live for themselves, but for Him who died and rose again on their behalf."

2. 1 John 2:1-2—"If anyone sins, we have an Advocate with the Father, Jesus Christ the righteous; and He Himself is the propitiation for our sins; and not for ours only, but also for those of the whole world." The Old Testament sacrifices were limited to a certain person, family, nation, or time. But the sacrifice of Christ was a propitiation for all sin, satisfying God's righteous requirement.

3. John 3:16—"God so loved the world, that He gave His only begotten Son, that whoever believes in Him should not perish, but have eternal life."

4. John 6:37-40—Jesus said, "All that the Father gives Me shall come to Me, and the one who comes to Me I will certainly not cast out. For I have come down from heaven, not to do My own will, but the will of Him who sent Me. And this is the will of Him who sent Me, that of all that He has given Me I lose nothing, but raise it up on the last day. For this is the will of My Father, that everyone who beholds the Son and believes in Him, may have eternal life."

Christ came to provide salvation for all who would come to Him.

E. Christ's Suffering Was Vicarious

Christ suffered as "the just for the unjust" (1 Pet. 3:18).

1. 1 Peter 2:24—Christ "bore our sins in His body on the cross, that we might die to sin and live to righteousness; for by His wounds you were healed."

2. 2 Corinthians 5:21—"He made Him who knew no sin . . . sin on our behalf, that we might become the righteousness of God in Him."

3. Hebrews 9:28—"Christ also, having been offered once to bear the sins of many, shall appear a second time for salvation without reference to sin, to those who eagerly await Him."

4. Acts 3:14-15—Peter said to those at the Temple in Jerusalem, "You disowned the Holy and Righteous One, and asked for a murderer to be granted to you, but put to death the Prince of life."

Christ, the holy and righteous One, took upon Himself the full penalty due the unrighteous. He was the perfect, full, and final sacrifice for sins. Even extreme suffering can be triumphant.

F. Christ's Suffering Was Purposeful

Christ died "in order that He might bring us to God, having been put to death in the flesh, but made alive in the spirit" (1 Pet. 3:18). Christ's purpose in gathering up our sins on the cross and enduring the darkness of death was to open the way to God. God demonstrated that truth symbolically by ripping the Temple veil from top to bottom, opening the Holy of Holies to immediate access by all worshipers (Matt. 27:51). As priests, all believers may come into the presence of God (1 Pet. 2:9; Heb. 4:16).

Hebrews 6:20 says that Jesus entered the heavenly Holy of Holies "as a [pioneer] for us, having become a high priest forever." He entered to bring the elect into communion with God. The Greek verb translated "He might bring" (*prosagō*; 1 Pet. 3:18) states the purpose of Jesus' actions. It was often used to describe someone's being introduced or provided access to another. The noun form of the word refers to the one making the introduction. There were officials in ancient courts who controlled access to the king. Once convinced of a person's right to access, the official would introduce that person into the king's presence. And that's exactly the function Jesus performs for us now. As He said, "No one comes to the Father, but through Me" (John 14:6; cf. Acts 4:12). He came to lead us into the Father's presence.

Conclusion

Jesus' suffering led to the triumph of bearing the sins of humanity. He's not a fairy godmother or a superpsychiatrist but the One who introduces men and women to God. Those He ushers into the Father's presence all have a loathing of their sin, a desire to be forgiven, and a longing to know God. Those attitudes are the work of God in drawing us to Christ (cf. John 6:44). A response to the gospel message thus begins with a transformation in attitude toward sin and ourselves.

Beyond that initial change in attitude is the transformation brought about in every believer at the instant of salvation. Christ didn't die just to pay the penalty for sin: He died to transform us.

Deserted by most of His followers, Christ hung in darkness and agony on the cross, crying out, "My God, My God, why hast Thou forsaken Me?" (Matt. 27:46). Those were moments of incredible rejection and hostility borne by our Lord. Yet out of those very circumstances He triumphed by atoning for sin and providing a way for men and women to be introduced to God and transformed. It was a triumph He Himself would soon proclaim (1 Pet. 3:19-20).

That triumph shows us that if we go through unjust suffering with the right attitude, it may lead to the salvation of others. It also shows us that if we suffer for righteousness' sake and commit ourselves to God, we too will triumph as Jesus did.

Focusing on the Facts

1. What is the theme of 1 Peter? Explain (see p. 38).

2. How did Peter show he was aware there were people who desired to harm his readers? What kinds of harm does Peter mention (see pp. 38-39)?
3. Suffering is to be a time of _____ and _____ for believers (see p. 40).
4. What is the key thought in 1 Peter 3:18-22 (see p. 40)?
5. How might God use our Christlike response to suffering (see p. 40)?
6. When the Lord asks us to suffer for His sake, we must realize we are being asked only to endure what _____ _____ _____ (see pp. 40-41).
7. For whose sins did Jesus die (see p. 41)?
8. What is the meaning of the Greek word *hapax*? In what way did that word express a new idea to Jewish people (see p. 42)?
9. The sacrifice of Christ was a propitiation for _____ _____ (see p. 43).
10. Christ suffered as the _____ for the _____ (see 1 Pet. 3:18; p. 43).
11. Christ's death shows that even extreme suffering can be _____ _____ (see p. 44).
12. What was Christ's purpose in gathering up our sins on the cross and enduring the darkness of death (see p. 44)?
13. What attitudes does God produce to draw a person to Christ (see p. 45)?

Pondering the Principles

1. A Christian can be content in the midst of suffering even as Christ "for the joy set before him endured the cross, scorning its shame" (Heb. 12:2; NIV). The Puritan Jeremiah Burroughs wrote, "Grace gives a man an eye, a piercing eye to pierce into the counsel of God, those eternal counsels of God for good to him, even in his afflictions; he can see the love of God in every affliction as well as in prosperity. Now this is a mystery to a carnal heart. They can see no such thing; perhaps they think God loves them when he prospers them and makes them rich, but they think God loves them not when he afflicts them. That is a mystery, but grace instructs men in that mystery, grace enables men to see love in the very frown of God's face, and so comes to receive contentment" (*The Rare Jewel of Christian Contentment* [Edinburgh:

Banner of Truth Trust, 1964 reprint], p. 60). Do you see with the eye of grace the value of suffering in your life?

2. Christians are not simply cleansed of their sin—they experience a drastic change in their relationship to God. Thomas Watson wrote, "It is one thing for a traitor to be pardoned, and another thing to be made a favourite. Christ's blood is not only called a sacrifice, whereby God is appeased, but a propitiation, whereby God becomes gracious and friendly to us" (*A Body of Divinity* [Edinburgh: Banner of Truth Trust, 1958 reprint], p. 174). If you claim a changed relationship to God through Christ, that's saying you are His friend and favorite—though once you were His enemy. When others examine your life, do they see a person who behaves as a friend and favorite of God?

5

The Triumph of Christ's Suffering— Part 2

Outline

Introduction

Review
I. The Triumph of Bearing the Sins of Humanity (v. 18*a*)

Lesson
II. The Triumph of Declaring Victory to the Enemy (vv. 18*b*-20*a*)
   A. The Condition of Christ's Spirit (v. 18*b*)
      1. The death of His flesh
      2. The life of His spirit
   B. The Journey Christ Made (v. 19*a*)
   C. The Proclamation Christ Gave (v. 19*b*)
   D. The Audience of Christ's Proclamation (v. 19*c*)
      1. Were they angels or men?
      2. Why did Christ preach to them?
   E. The Imprisonment of Christ's Audience (v. 19*d*)
   F. The Sin of Christ's Audience (v. 20*a*)
      1. They overstepped their bounds
      2. Their sin was well-known
      3. They went after "strange flesh"
      4. They attempted to thwart God's plan of salvation

Conclusion

Introduction

The suffering of Christ on the cross was both His greatest humiliation and greatest triumph. The apostle Peter wrote his first epistle to encourage believers who were undergoing severe persecutions and trials. He pointed to Christ as the supreme example of the triumph that comes through suffering in the will of God.

First Peter 3:18-22 says that Christ "also died for sins once for all, the just for the unjust, in order that He might bring us to God, having been put to death in the flesh, but made alive in the spirit; in which also He went and made proclamation to the spirits now in prison, who once were disobedient, when the patience of God kept waiting in the days of Noah, during the construction of the ark, in which a few, that is, eight persons, were brought safely through the water. And corresponding to that, baptism now saves you—not the removal of dirt from the flesh, but an appeal to God for a good conscience—through the resurrection of Jesus Christ, who is at the right hand of God, having gone into heaven, after angels and authorities and powers had been subjected to Him."

The thrust of that key passage is its beginning, "Christ . . . died," and ending, "Angels and authorities and powers had been subjected to Him." Peter's message is that though we might suffer unjustly and severely as our Lord did, God will provide victory in the end. Verses 18-22 highlight the triumph of Christ's bearing the sins of humanity, declaring His victory to the enemy, saving His people from destruction, and reigning supreme over all.

Review

I. THE TRIUMPH OF BEARING THE SINS OF HUMANITY (v. 18a; see pp. 40-45)

"Christ . . . died for sins once for all, the just for the unjust, in order that He might bring us to God."

II. THE TRIUMPH OF DECLARING VICTORY TO THE ENEMY
(vv. 18*b*-20)

"[Christ was] put to death in the flesh, but made alive in the
spirit; in which also He went and made proclamation to the
spirits now in prison, who once were disobedient, when the
patience of God kept waiting in the days of Noah."

A. The Condition of Christ's Spirit (v. 18*b*)

"[Christ was] put to death in the flesh, but made alive in
the spirit."

1. The death of His flesh

The phrase "put to death in the flesh" means that
Christ's physical life ceased. Some dispute the resurrection of Christ from the dead by claiming that He
never died but only fainted. Supposedly He was re-
vived by the coolness of His tomb, got up, and walked
out. But Peter is clear: Jesus was dead—the victim
of a judicial murder.

The term Peter used (Gk., *thanatoō*) means "to die."
Thanatology is the study of death. Beyond that basic
meaning, the word also carries the connotation of
violence. Here it emphasizes the suffering associated
with the violent death of Christ.

Christ's Roman executioners were sure He was dead.
They broke the legs of the thieves crucified alongside
of Him to hasten their deaths (a victim of crucifixion
could postpone death as long as he could elevate
himself on his legs). However, they didn't bother to
break Christ's legs since they could see He was al-
ready dead. To verify that they pierced His side, out
of which came a flow of blood and water (John 19:31-
37). Christ was surely dead.

2. The life of His spirit

The phrase "made alive in the spirit" refers to the life of Jesus' spirit—not to the Holy Spirit. There's no article in the Greek text indicating that Peter was referring to the Holy Spirit. Rather, he seems to be contrasting what happened to the flesh (or body) of Jesus with what happened to His spirit. His spirit was alive, but His flesh was dead.

Some think "made alive in the spirit" refers to Christ's resurrection, but that would necessitate a statement such as, "He was put to death in the flesh but made alive in the flesh." The resurrection was a spiritual *and* physical occurrence. Thus Peter's point has to be that though Christ was physically dead, His spirit was still alive.

Though in spirit Christ was alive, He did experience spiritual death—not cessation of existence but separation from God. On the cross He said, "My God, My God, why hast Thou forsaken Me?" (Matt. 27:46). That shows the separation He temporarily experienced from the Father when He was made sin for us (2 Cor. 5:21). Similarly, unbelievers experience spiritual death (separation from God) in this life and eternal death in the next, but they never cease to exist.

The separation between Christ and the Father was over quickly, for shortly after our Lord's lament He said, "Father, into Thy hands I commit My spirit" (Luke 23:46). That shows His spirit was alive again—no longer separated from God—and could be committed to the Father.

B. The Journey Christ Made (v. 19a)

"In which also He went."

After the crucifixion Christ's body was laid in a tomb. "In which also" points to what happened to Christ's living spirit. While Christ's body lay in the tomb, He went in His spirit to another place.

The Greek verb translated "He went" (*poreuomai*) refers to going from one place to another (cf. v. 22). Unlike the spirits of the unrighteous, who immediately experience the wrath of God after death, the spirit of Christ was able to accomplish God's perfect purpose.

C. The Proclamation Christ Gave (v. 19*b*)

"[He] made proclamation."

Christ went to preach a triumphant sermon before His resurrection Sunday morning. The verb translated "made proclamation" (*kērussō*) refers to making a proclamation or announcing a triumph. In ancient times a herald would precede generals and kings in the celebration of military victories, announcing to all the victories won in battle. That's what Jesus went to do—He didn't go to preach the gospel (Gk., *euangelizō*, "to evangelize") but to announce His triumph over sin, death, hell, demons, and Satan. He didn't go to win souls but to proclaim victory to the enemy in spite of the unjust suffering they subjected Him to.

D. The Audience of Christ's Proclamation (v. 19*c*)

"[He proclaimed] to the spirits."

1. Were they angels or men?

    Verse 20 speaks of "persons" (Gk., *psuchai*, "souls"), whereas verse 19 speaks of "spirits" (*pneumasin*). Peter was referring to two different kinds of beings: human beings in verse 20 and spirit beings, or angels, in verse 19. Another thing indicating that verse 19 doesn't refer to human beings is that the New Testament never uses "spirits" to refer to humans except when qualified by a genitive (e.g., Hebrews 12:23, which reads "to the spirits *of righteous men*").

    A final clue for determining that verse 19 refers to angels is that verse 22 says Jesus "is at the right hand of God, having gone into heaven, after angels and authorities and powers had been subjected to Him."

53

"Angels and authorities and powers" all refer to angelic beings.

The angels Jesus made proclamation to were not just any angels—they were demons said to be "in prison" (v. 19). That shows Jesus wasn't preaching a message of salvation, since demons can't be saved: they're damned forever. As Hebrews 2:16 says, "[Christ] does not give help to angels, but He gives help to the descendant of Abraham."

2. Why did Christ preach to them?

Christ proclaimed victory over the enemy. Since the beginning of time Satan and his cohorts have been at war with God. We see that cosmic conflict reflected many times in Scripture (e.g., Job 1; Daniel 10:13). After Satan's apparent triumph in bringing about the Fall of mankind, God predicted his eventual destruction by the Messiah, who would triumph ultimately in spite of a seeming setback (Gen. 3:15). As a result Satan attempted to destroy the messianic line by destroying God's people. When that failed he tried to slaughter the infant Messiah (Matt. 2:16-18). When that didn't work he attempted to corrupt the Messiah (Matt. 4:1-11; Luke 4:1-13). Failure in that attempt caused him to instigate mobs to kill Him. He even tried to make sure the Messiah couldn't come forth from the tomb. It's been said that hell must have been in the midst of a carnival when He arrived. They were probably celebrating the victory they had tried so hard to secure—but they were abruptly disappointed.

E. The Imprisonment of Christ's Audience (v. 19d)

"[He proclaimed] in prison."

Scripture never describes the souls of dead men as being in prison. Yet these spirits, or angels, are in a specific location: a *phulakē* or place of imprisonment.

Not all demons are imprisoned. There are two kinds of angels: holy angels and fallen angels (demons). There are two kinds of demons: those who are bound and those who are not. Of the bound demons there are two kinds: those temporarily bound and those permanently bound. Jesus went to where those permanently bound are imprisoned.

What We Struggle Against

Ephesians 6:12 says, "Our struggle is not against flesh and blood, but against the rulers, against the powers, against the world forces of this darkness, against the spiritual forces of wickedness in the heavenly places." That's the struggle believers have against demons who aren't bound. Luke 8:31 says that the demons in a man named Legion (many demons were in him) "were entreating Him [Jesus] not to command them to depart into the abyss." Matthew 8:29 records that they said, "What do we have to do with You, Son of God? Have You come here to torment us before the time?" The demons who are free are terrified of the judgment that awaits them.

F. The Sin of Christ's Audience (v. 20a)

"[They] once were disobedient, when the patience of God kept waiting in the days of Noah."

1. They overstepped their bounds

The demons to whom Christ proclaimed victory had been disobedient during the time of Noah. They were sent to prison because they overstepped the bounds established for them by God.

The Sermon of the Ark

God commanded Noah to build an ark—a great boat (Gen. 6:13-17). Whereas it did serve to rescue Noah and his family from the judgment of the Flood, its main purpose was to serve as a sermon. It took 120 years to build, and all that time it served as an object lesson of the impending judgment of God. Yet none but Noah's family heeded the warning of the ark, and all drowned but them.

55

The wickedness of Noah's day shows the lack of responsiveness to the sermon of the ark. Genesis 6:5 says, "The Lord saw that the wickedness of man was great on the earth, and that every intent of the thoughts of his heart was only evil continually." It was a time of great demonic activity, prompting God to drown the whole earth.

2. Their sin was well-known

The specific sin committed by the bound demons must have been well-known to Peter's readers since Peter's mention of it is so cursory. He would otherwise have gone into greater detail to explain what he was talking about.

Second Peter 2:4-5 also refers to those demons in a cursory way: "God did not spare angels when they sinned, but cast them into hell and committed them to pits of darkness, reserved for judgment; and did not spare the ancient world, but preserved Noah, a preacher of righteousness, with seven others, when He brought a flood upon the world of the ungodly." The following verses refer to the condemnation of Sodom and Go-morrah (vv. 6-8). Each of those occurrences are de-scribed in Genesis (Gen. 6, 18-19), and it is logical to assume that both occurrences involved the same sin.

Why Did Peter's Readers Know so Much About Fallen Angels?

The phrase translated "cast them into hell" in 2 Peter 2:4 is the Greek verb *tartaroō*, which means "to consign to Tartarus." According to classical Greek mythology, Tartarus is the subterranean abyss in which rebellious gods are punished. It was adopted in Judaism to describe the prison of fallen angels.

Tartarus is also mentioned in the pseudepigraphal book of Enoch (Enoch 20:2), a familiar book to Jewish people of New Testament times. The epistle of Jude refers to it (Jude 14; cf. Enoch 1:9). The book of Enoch indicates that certain angels overstepped their bounds, referring to their sin in the same way Peter's letters do. Apparently Peter knew his audience was aware of the book of

Enoch, so he had only to mention the fall of the angels and their incarceration in Tartarus for his readers to know exactly what he was talking about.

3. They went after "strange flesh"

The epistle of Jude says the "angels who did not keep their own domain, but abandoned their proper abode, He [God] has kept in eternal bonds under darkness for the judgment of the great day. Just as Sodom and Gomorrah and the cities around them, since they in the same way as these indulged in gross immorality and went after strange flesh, are exhibited as an example, in undergoing the punishment of eternal fire" (6-7). That describes the eternal incarceration of angels who overstepped their bounds and also specifies the kind of sin they committed: the sin of Sodom and Gomorrah—going after "strange flesh."

In Sodom and Gomorrah homosexuality was rampant. When angels visited Lot (Gen. 19), the homosexual men of Sodom came to his house and tried to break in and rape the angels. Even when struck blind by the angels, the men were so crazed with lust that they still tried to get to them. Whatever the angels who are bound in Tartarus did, it was similar to that sin.

Genesis 6:1-4 says, "When men began to multiply on the face of the land, and daughters were born to them . . . the sons of God saw that the daughters of men were beautiful; and they took wives for themselves, whomever they chose. Then the Lord said, 'My Spirit shall not strive with man forever, because he also is flesh; nevertheless his days shall be one hundred and twenty years.' The Nephilim were on the earth in those days, and also afterward, when the sons of God came in to the daughters of men, and they bore children to them. Those were the mighty men who were of old, men of renown."

That's a description of demons who assumed human form and cohabitated with women, producing a demon hybrid race. That race may have been the Nephilim

57

mentioned in Genesis 6:4. Nephilim is derived from the Hebrew verb *naphal*, which means "to fall." It can refer to those who are violent and in Numbers 13:33 refers to people of great size. Genesis 6:4 describes them as "mighty men" and "men of renown." Apparently that hybrid race was powerful, large, and violent.

4. They attempted to thwart God's plan of salvation

The race produced through the sin of the bound demons was unredeemable. That's because Christ, the God/man, came to save man—not demon/man. That sin was a deliberate attempt to corrupt the entire human race and thwart the plan of salvation. As a result it was necessary to destroy the whole earth with water to prevent total corruption of the human race.

What About Those "Sons of God" in Genesis 6?

Some think the "sons of God" mentioned in Genesis 6 refers to the descendants of Seth, a son of Adam (Gen. 5:3). They say the text is describing the intermingling of believers (the descendants of Seth) and non-believers. But there are a number of reasons that the phrase "sons of God" is better understood as a reference to fallen angels (or demons):

1. It is the oldest view and was widely held in antiquity (see Gordon J. Wenham, *Genesis 1-15*, Word Biblical Commentary, vol. 1 [Waco: Word Books, 1987], p. 139).

2. The specific phrase "sons of God" (Heb., *bene haelohim*) always refers to angels in its other Old Testament usages.

3. Some manuscripts of the Greek Old Testament (the Septuagint) translate *bene haelohim* as "angels."

4. The specific phrase "sons of God" is always used to refer to those brought directly into being by God—not those who are procreated through human birth.

5. The early church held this view until the fourth century A.D.

6. If the phrase "sons of God" refers only to Sethites, all Sethites must have been male since they are said to have taken wives from the "daughters of men" (Gen. 6:2).

7. If the phrase "sons of God" only refers to men, it would have been simpler to say that the sons of men took wives from the daughters of men.

8. If the "sons of God" were believers, they also perished in the Flood, and that would contradict 2 Peter 2:5.

9. If only human intermarriage is in view here, it is difficult to understand why that brought on such fearful judgment (the Flood), especially since there is no condemnation of marriage between believers and non-believers in Genesis 1-6.

Conclusion

The demons who overstepped their bounds have been in prison a long time. When Jesus died on the cross, perhaps they thought He had been robbed of the keys to their prison—but He hadn't. Instead He appeared before them personally and proclaimed His triumph.

Colossians 2:15 says, "When [God] had disarmed the rulers and authorities, He made a public display of them, having triumphed over them through [Christ]." I believe that's referring to the same thing 1 Peter 3:19-20 refers to. At the cross Jesus experienced unjust suffering and terrible persecution. Yet through it He bore the sins of humanity and then went to preach His triumph over sin, Satan, hell, demons, and death. What an example of passing through suffering to triumph!

Focusing on the Facts

1. Why did the apostle Peter write his first epistle (see p. 50)?
2. What's the thrust of 1 Peter 3:18-22? What is the overall message (see p. 50)?
3. Did Christ really die a physical death on the cross? Explain (see p. 51).

4. What does the phrase "made alive in the spirit" refer to (1 Peter 3:18; see p. 52)?
5. In what sense did Christ experience spiritual death (see p. 52)?
6. Unlike the spirits of the unrighteous who immediately experience the wrath of God after death, the spirit of Christ was able to _____ _____ _____ _____ (see p. 53).
7. What did Christ go to do before His resurrection Sunday morning (see p. 53)?
8. To whom did Christ speak in 1 Peter 3:19 (see pp. 53-54)?
9. Where did He speak (see pp. 54-55)?
10. Why was Jesus' audience where they were (see p. 55)?
11. What was the main purpose of the ark Noah built (see p. 55)?
12. How could Peter's readers have known so much about what he describes in 1 Peter 3:20 (see pp. 56-57)?
13. What was the sin of Sodom and Gomorrah for which those described in 1 Peter 3:20 were imprisoned (see p. 57)?
14. What does Genesis 6:1-4 indicate about the sin of those described in 1 Peter 3:20? What was the result of that sin (see pp. 57-58)?
15. Who are the "sons of God" in Genesis 6 (see pp. 58-59)?

Pondering the Principles

1. The death of Christ on behalf of sinners was an act of grace. British theologian A. W. Pink wrote how helpful it was for him to realize that "grace is something more than 'unmerited favor.' To feed a tramp who calls on me is 'unmerited favor,' but it is scarcely grace. But suppose that after he has robbed me I should feed this starving tramp—that would be 'grace.' Grace, then, is favour shown where there is positive de-merit in the one receiving it" (*The Sovereignty of God*, revised ed. [Edinburgh: Banner of Truth Trust, 1961], p. 25). Christ did not die for sinful angels, but He did die for sinful men and women. Be grateful that "while we were still helpless at the right time Christ died for the ungodly" (Rom. 5:6).

2. In his hymn "And Can It Be That I Should Gain," Charles Wesley wrote,

'Tis mystery all! Th' Immortal dies!
Who can explore His strange design?
In vain the first born seraph tries
To sound the depths of love Divine!
'Tis mercy all! let earth adore,
Let angel minds inquire no more.

It was lost *man* whom Christ bled for—the lost angels could only listen in dismay to Christ's proclamation of victory. Unlike fallen mankind, the fallen angels cannot participate in the atoning work of Christ, and the elect angels can only marvel at what they cannot fully understand (1 Pet. 1:12). Take time now to praise God for making you a man or woman who can participate in the work of Christ on the cross—and not an angel!

6

The Triumph of Christ's Suffering— Part 3

Outline

Introduction

Review
I.   The Triumph of Bearing the Sins of Humanity (v. 18*a*)
II. The Triumph of Declaring Victory to the Enemy (v. 18*b*-20*a*)
A. The Condition of Christ's Spirit (v. 18*b*)
B. The Journey Christ Made (v. 19*a*)
C. The Proclamation Christ Gave (v. 19*b*)
D. The Audience of Christ's Proclamation (v. 19*c*)
E. The Imprisonment of Christ's Audience (v. 19*d*)
F. The Sin of Christ's Audience (v. 20*a*)

Lesson
III. The Triumph of Saving His People from Destruction (vv. 20*b*-21)
A. The Ark (v. 20*b*)
B. The Antitype (v. 21)
1. What it is
2. What it is not
3. What it describes
   a) Believers are safe in Christ
   b) Believers are entombed in Christ
4. How it applies to us
IV. The Triumph in Reigning Supreme over All (v. 22)
A. Christ's Position
B. Christ's Ascension

C. Christ's Work
D. Christ's Supremacy

Conclusion

Introduction

The time of our Lord's greatest suffering was the time of His greatest triumph. The lesson for us is not to despair when enduring difficulty, rejection, persecution, and unjust treatment—it may be the time of our greatest triumph. Peter wrote to encourage believers in difficult circumstances, and that includes us.

First Peter 3:18-22 says, "Christ . . . died for sins once for all, the just for the unjust, in order that He might bring us to God, having been put to death in the flesh, but made alive in the spirit; in which also He went and made proclamation to the spirits now in prison, who once were disobedient, when the patience of God kept waiting in the days of Noah, during the construction of the ark, in which a few, that is, eight persons, were brought safely through the water. And corresponding to that, baptism now saves you—not the removal of dirt from the flesh, but an appeal to God for a good conscience—through the resurrection of Jesus Christ, who is at the right hand of God, having gone into heaven, after angels and authorities and powers had been subjected to Him."

Review

I. THE TRIUMPH OF BEARING THE SINS OF HUMANITY
(v. 18a; see pp. 40-45)

"Christ . . . died for sins once for all, the just for the unjust, in order that He might bring us to God."

64

II. THE TRIUMPH OF DECLARING VICTORY TO THE EN-
EMY (v. 18*b*-20*a*)

"[Christ was] put to death in the flesh, but made alive in the
spirit; in which also He went and made proclamation to the
spirits now in prison, who once were disobedient, when the
patience of God kept waiting in the days of Noah."

A. The Condition of Christ's Spirit (v. 18*b*; see pp. 51-52)

B. The Journey Christ Made (v. 19*a*; see pp. 52-53)

C. The Proclamation Christ Gave (v. 19*b*; see p. 53)

D. The Audience of Christ's Proclamation (v. 19*c*; see pp. 53-
54)

E. The Imprisonment of Christ's Audience (v. 19*d*; see pp.
54-55)

F. The Sin of Christ's Audience (v. 20*a*; see pp. 55-59)

Some wonder how demons could have cohabited with
women since Matthew 22:30 says, "In the resurrection
[God's children] neither marry, nor are given in marriage,
but are like angels in heaven." It would seem that
because angels do not marry, they do not procreate. But
that's what made the sin referred to in 1 Peter 3:20 so
heinous: because the angels now in prison could not
procreate among themselves, they assumed a human form
and did so with women, thus corrupting the human race.
Matthew 22:30 refers to the angels in heaven—not of
what happened when some of them left their proper
domain and cohabited with women.

There seems to be a correlation between demonic activity
(whether Satanism, witchcraft, or the occult) and perverted sex. That's nothing new—it's as old as the sin of
the demons to whom Christ proclaimed His victory.

Lesson

III. THE TRIUMPH OF SAVING HIS PEOPLE FROM DESTRUC-
TION (vv. 20b-21)

"[God was patient in the days of Noah] during the construction of the ark, in which a few, that is, eight persons, were
brought safely through the water. And corresponding to
that, baptism now saves you—not the removal of dirt from the
flesh but an appeal to God for a good conscience—through
the resurrection of Jesus Christ."

A. The Ark (v. 20b)

"[God was patient in the days of Noah] during the construction of the ark, in which a few, that is, eight persons,
were brought safely through the water."

Peter used the historical account of Noah and his family
as an analogy for the triumphant salvation provided
through Christ. Genesis 6:9–8:22 tells how Noah and his
family were delivered through the Flood. They were the
only people who believed God's warning of the coming
worldwide catastrophe. As a result all mankind was drowned in judgment, except them.

It's remarkable that so few believed God's warning—
Noah, "a preacher of righteousness" (2 Pet. 2:5), preached
the righteousness of God for the hundred and twenty
years it took to build the ark. It was a massive structure
about the size of a modern ocean liner (Gen. 6:15) and
was sure to attract attention. Yet that tremendous effort
was spent on building a vessel he would spend only a
year using. Imagine what it would be like to build that
ark and preach its meaning for more than a century, yet
have only your immediate family believe. It must have
been discouraging. Yet those were the people who were
safe from God's judgment when the rains did come. The
ark carried them from a world of wickedness and iniquity
(Gen. 6:5) into a new world and life. The ark served as
their shelter from the encompassing judgment of God. For
Peter the experience of Noah and his family was a graphic
illustration of salvation.

B. The Antitype (v. 21)

"And corresponding to that, baptism now saves you—not the removal of dirt from the flesh, but an appeal to God for a good conscience—through the resurrection of Jesus Christ."

"And corresponding to that" translates a Greek phrase containing the word *antitupon,* which means "antitype" or "copy." In the New Testament it describes an earthly expression of a heavenly reality—a symbol, copy, or analogy of a spiritual truth. Peter understood the preservation of the believers in the ark to be symbolic of salvation in Christ.

1. What it is

Some believe that the antitype Peter speaks of is the water of the Flood because the Greek words for "antitype" (v. 21) and "water" (v. 20) are both neuter gender words in Greek. But it seems better to understand the antitype to be the whole experience of Noah and his family: the preservation of believers in an ark while the earth was immersed in the judgment of God. That would make Noah and his family a true antitype of salvation in Christ, which is a preservation through judgment.

2. What it is not

The baptism Peter speaks of in verse 21 is not water baptism. The Greek word translated "baptism" (*baptizō*) is more specifically translated "immerse." Noah didn't experience Christian baptism but was immersed in judgment though protected by the ark. Noah and his family didn't miss the judgment—they were there—but were preserved through it. That's what happens to believers in Christ.

Peter made especially clear he wasn't talking about Christian baptism when he said, "Not the removal of dirt from the flesh." He wasn't speaking of an earthly ordinance but a spiritual reality: "an appeal to God for a good conscience—through the resurrection of Jesus Christ" (v. 21).

3. What it describes

a) Believers are safe in Christ

"Not the removal of dirt from the flesh, but an appeal to God for a good conscience" qualifies the statement "baptism now saves you." Without that qualifying phrase verse 21 reads, "Baptism now saves you through the resurrection of Jesus Christ." The only baptism that saves a person is one into the death and resurrection of Jesus Christ.

Peter's point is that just as the Flood immersed everyone in the judgment of God, yet some passed through safely, so the final judgment will fall on all, but those who are in Jesus Christ will pass through safely. Being in Christ is like being in the ark: we ride safely through the storms of judgment. Believers go through the death and burial of Christ because of their union with Him and come out again into the new world of His resurrection.

b) Believers are entombed in Christ

The ark of Noah was a kind of tomb—those in it died to their world when they entered it. When they left it atop Mount Ararat, they experienced a resurrection of sorts by entering a new world. That, Peter tells us, is analogous to the experience of every Christian: spiritually we enter Christ and die to the world we come from, and one day we will be resurrected for a new world and life. That's similar to what Paul said in Romans 6:3-4: "Do you not know that all of us who have been baptized into Christ Jesus have been baptized into His death? Therefore we have been buried with Him through baptism into death, in order that as Christ was raised from the dead through the glory of the Father, so we too might walk in newness of life."

Alan Stibbs wrote, "The ark passing safely through the flood provides a figure of God's method of saving men out of inevitable judgment. First, God delayed the day of judgment long enough for an ark to be prepared. Then, the souls that went into the ark did not avoid the judgment. Rather in the ark they were saved through the very water which drowned others, and, because of it, they thus passed out of the old world into a new world. When they emerged from the ark they literally found that old things had passed away, and all things were become new.

"This figure is fulfilled in Christ. . . . He was prepared of God to come in the fulness of time. The judgment due to sin and sinners was meanwhile delayed. Then the judgment fell upon Him, as the flood waters upon the ark. When sinners take refuge in Him, they do not avoid the judgment due to sin, they are saved through its falling upon Christ; and, because of it, instead of meeting their own doom, are brought safe unto God" (*The First Epistle of Peter* [Grand Rapids: Eerdmans, 1971], pp. 139-40).

4. How it applies to us

Our safety in Christ comes not by "the removal of dirt from the flesh" (water baptism) but by "an appeal to God for a good conscience" (v. 21). The Greek word translated "appeal" (*eperōtēma*) was a technical term used in making a contract. Here it refers to agreeing to meet certain conditions required by God before being placed into the ark of safety (Christ). Salvation requires the desire to obtain a cleansed conscience from God and a willingness to meet the conditions necessary to obtain it.

Unregenerate men and women have consciences that condemn them. One who appeals to God for a good conscience is sick of his sin and desires to be delivered from the load of guilt he bears. He has a crushing and intimidating fear of coming judgment and knows that only God can deliver him. He desires the cleansing that comes through the blood of Christ (cf. Heb. 9:14; 10:22). So he repents of his sin and pleads for forgiveness. It's not baptism that saves, but the security of being placed safely in Jesus Christ—our ark of salvation.

Who Got Wet?

Some time ago I read a book in which the writer discussed the interpretation that 1 Peter 3:21 says people are saved by water baptism: "I once asked a Mormon elder, who advanced this idea, if he would please tell me who were baptized in Noah's day—the saved or the lost? Not a drop of water touched Noah and his family; all those who went into the water of baptism were drowned. It puzzled him a bit and he replied, 'Then, what does it mean when it says they were saved by water?' The answer is that it means just what it says. They were saved by water, but not the water that fell on them, for none fell on them. They were saved by the water that fell on the ark. The water burst from beneath (typical of man's hatred and wickedness that nailed the Son of God to the cross), and the waters came from above (typical of the judgment from above which our blessed Saviour bore on the cross). Yes, those waters typify the waves and billows of judgment which lifted Christ—our Ark of safety—up on the cross. It is by that redemptive work that we are saved. Those waters of judgment fell on Him; not on us. Like Noah and his family we who are believers are safe and secure in Christ. We are saved by the baptism of judgment Christ knew at Calvary; not by the baptism of water. The text in 1 Peter does not say we are saved by baptism. It says that baptism is a like figure. Both Noah's ark and baptism prefigure the same thing; they picture the work of Christ as He bore our sins and rose victoriously from the dead" (August Van Ryn, *Acts of the Apostles* [N.Y.: Loizeaux Bros., 1961], pp. 42-43).

When Christ suffered on the cross, hell threw all its fury at Him and wicked men vented their hatred on Him. Yet through that suffering He served as an ark of safety for the redeemed of all ages. He went through judgment without allowing a drop to touch any who are in Him. And because He triumphantly provided salvation through His suffering we are safe in Him through judgment and will emerge in a new world through His resurrection.

70

IV. THE TRIUMPH IN REIGNING SUPREME OVER ALL (v. 22)

"[Christ] is at the right hand of God, having gone into heaven, after angels and authorities and powers had been subjected to Him."

After describing all the suffering Christ endured, Peter ends this section of Scripture in a glorious final note of triumph. Throughout both the Old and New Testaments, the right hand of God is affirmed as the place of preeminence, power, and authority for all eternity. That's where Jesus went when He had accomplished His work on the cross, and that's where He rules from today.

A. Christ's Position

1. Hebrews 1:3-6—"[Jesus Christ] is the radiance of His [God's] glory and the exact representation of His nature, and upholds all things by the word of His power. When He had made purification of sins, He sat down at the right hand of the Majesty on high; having become as much better than the angels, as He has inherited a more excellent name than they. For to which of the angels did He ever say, 'Thou art My Son, Today I have begotten Thee'? And again, 'I will be a Father to Him and He shall be a Son to Me'? And when He again brings the first-born into the world, He says, 'And let all the angels of God worship Him.'"

2. Hebrews 10:12—"[Jesus], having offered one sacrifice for sins for all time, sat down at the right hand of God."

3. Hebrews 12:2—We are to be "fixing our eyes on Jesus, the author and perfecter of faith, who for the joy set before Him endured the cross, despising the shame, and has sat down at the right hand of the throne of God."

4. Romans 8:34—"Christ Jesus is He who died, yes, rather who was raised, who is at the right hand of God, who also intercedes for us." His position at the

right hand of God gives Him authority over all created things.

5. Philippians 2:9-11—After describing how Jesus suffered, Paul then said that "God highly exalted Him, and bestowed on Him the name which is above every name, that at the name of Jesus every knee should bow, of those who are in heaven, and on earth, and under the earth, and that every tongue should confess that Jesus Christ is Lord, to the glory of God the Father."

B. Christ's Ascension

Christ came to the right hand of God, "having gone into heaven" (1 Pet. 3:22)—a reference to His ascension.

1. Acts 1:9-11—"He was lifted up while they were looking on, and a cloud received Him out of their sight. And as they were gazing intently into the sky while He was departing, behold, two men in white clothing stood beside them; and they also said, 'Men of Galilee, why do you stand looking into the sky? This Jesus, who has been taken up from you into heaven, will come in just the same way as you have watched Him go into heaven.'"

2. Hebrews 6:20—At His ascension "Jesus . . . entered as a forerunner for us, having become a high priest forever according to the order of Melchizedek."

C. Christ's Work

Christ now intercedes for us as our High Priest.

1. Hebrews 8:1—"We have . . . a high priest, who has taken His seat at the right hand of the throne of the Majesty in the heavens." That's the position from which He intercedes for us.

2. Hebrews 9:24—"Christ did not enter a holy place made with hands, a mere copy of the true one, but into heaven itself, now to appear in the presence of God for us."

D. Christ's Supremacy

Christ assumed His position of supremacy "after angels and authorities and powers had been subjected to Him" (1 Pet. 3:22). That refers to when Christ declared His triumph to the demons in prison. It clarifies that the cross and the resurrection are what subjected the angelic hosts (*angels, authorities,* and *powers* are all descriptive of angelic beings) to Him. That's Paul's point in Ephesians 1:20-21: "[God] raised Him [Christ] from the dead, and seated Him at His right hand in the heavenly places, far above all *rule* and *authority* and *power* and *dominion,* and every name that is named, not only in this age, but also in the one to come" (italics added). First Peter 3:22 uses the Greek word *hupotassō* ("to be lined up in rank under") to describe the present status of the angels in relation to Christ. He is supreme over all.

Conclusion

Christ triumphed through unjust suffering. Peter's point in showing us that great truth is to exhort us to follow the same path into glory. Paul made the same point:

• Romans 8:17—We are children and heirs of God "and fellow heirs with Christ, if indeed we suffer with Him in order that we may also be glorified with Him."

• 2 Timothy 2:10—"For this reason I endure all things for the sake of those who are chosen, that they also may obtain the salvation which is in Christ Jesus and with it eternal glory. It is a trustworthy statement: For if we died with Him, we shall also live with Him; if we endure, we shall also reign with Him." The path to glory is always through suffering.

• Philippians 1:29—To us "it has been granted for Christ's sake, not only to believe in Him, but also to suffer for His sake."

• 2 Corinthians 2:14—"Thanks be to God, who always leads us in His triumph in Christ, and manifests through us the sweet aroma of the knowledge of Him in every place." Christ will always cause us to triumph even though we suffer unjustly.

73

Don't underestimate the potential of unjust suffering for Christ's sake.

There are many possibilities that arise out of unjust suffering for Christ's sake. God may use your suffering to lead someone to Christ. He may use it to help you triumph over demonic persecution. It may enable another who sees your godly response to persecution to respond in the same way. Whatever the triumph of your suffering, you may be sure of one thing: if you suffer for Christ's sake, God will lift you up and exalt you into His very presence. So endure whatever suffering comes your way in the light of your coming triumph in Christ!

Focusing on the Facts

1. The time of our Lord's greatest suffering was also the time of His greatest _____ (see p. 64).
2. Does Matthew 22:30 mean that because angels don't marry they can't procreate? Why or why not (see p. 65)?
3. What did Noah do while building the ark (2 Pet. 2:5)? What was the response (see p. 66)?
4. What did the ark serve as for Noah and his family (see p. 66)?
5. How is the Greek word *antitupon* used in the New Testament (see p. 67)?
6. How does the experience of Noah and his family parallel salvation in Christ (see p. 67)?
7. Is 1 Peter 3:21 speaking of water baptism? Why or why not (see pp. 67-68)?
8. What is the baptism that saves a person (see p. 68)?
9. In what way can Jesus be said to be like an ark (see p. 68)?
10. In entering the ark, Noah and his family entered into a kind of tomb. How is that analogous to the experience of believers (see pp. 68-69)?
11. How does the Greek word *eperōtēma* describe the believer's relationship to God through Christ (see p. 69)?
12. What is characteristic of the consciences of unregenerate men and women? What has happened when a person appeals to God for a good conscience (see pp. 69-70)?
13. Because Christ triumphantly provided salvation through His suffering, we are _____ (see p. 70).

14. Where is Christ now? What is the significance of that (see pp. 71-72)?
15. How did Christ arrive at His present position? What is one way in which He represents us there (see p. 72)?
16. Who are the angels, authorities, and powers Peter refers to in 1 Peter 3:22? In what relationship does Christ stand to them (see p. 73)?
17. In what ways may we triumph through suffering (see pp. 73-74)?

Pondering the Principles

1. In *The Almost Christian Discovered* the Puritan Matthew Mead shows the extent to which a person can apparently suffer for Christ without actually being in Christ (Beaver Falls, Penn.: Soli Deo Gloria, n.d., pp. 97-98):

   - A person may suffer not because he belongs to Christ, but because he is religious.
   - A person may suffer on Christ's behalf yet have no love for Him.
   - A person may suffer thinking it will ingratiate himself to God.
   - A person may suffer not to glorify God but to benefit himself materially by association with God's people.
   - A person may suffer because of the opinions he holds rather than his relationship to Christ.

   Often when we suffer we take comfort in the fact that Jesus said we would suffer—and that's a good thing to do. However, the fact that a person can seemingly suffer in Christ's name yet not be a Christian ought to make us reflect on precisely what we are suffering for. Look at your life: Are you suffering for Christ's sake or because of your own thoughts, attitudes, and behavior? The triumph that comes through suffering comes only to those who suffer because of their relationship to Christ. When you suffer, make sure it's for the right reason.

2. Puritan pastor John Flavel said to reason this way before committing to Christ as Savior and Lord: "If I open to Christ, this I shall gain, but that I must lose; I cannot sep-

arate Christ from sufferings: Christ will separate me from my sins; if I seek him, I must let them go; if I profess Christ, Providence will one time or other bring me to this dilemma, either Christ or earthly comforts must go. It is necessary, therefore, that I now propound to myself what Providence may, one time or other, propound to me. He hath set down his terms: 'If any man will come after me, let him deny himself, and take up his cross and follow me.' " (*Christ Knocking at the Door of Sinners' Hearts* [Grand Rapids: Baker, 1978 reprint], p. 183). God will accept "an appeal to God for a good conscience" (1 Pet. 3:21) only on His terms. That requires a willingness to walk as Jesus walked and suffer as He did. Have you counted the cost and found yourself willing?

Scripture Index

Topical Index

Angels
 fallen. *See* Demons
 procreation and, 65
 salvation not available to,
  60-61
Ark, Noah's
 sermon of, 55-56
 symbolism behind, 66-70
Arrowsmith, John, on the
  sufferings of Chris-
  tians vs. non-Chris-
  tians, 12
Atonement, the, 40-45. *See
  also* Substitution
 completion of, 42-43
 extent of, 30-31, 43
 healing in, 33

Baptism, symbolism of, 67-70
Burroughs, Jeremiah, on contentment amidst suf-
  fering, 46-47

Catholicism, the mass, 42-43
Chambers, Oswald, on
  Christ's willingness to
  suffer, 36

Demons
 bound vs. unbound, 54-55
 Christ's proclamation to, 51-
  59
 pre-Flood, 55-59
 victory of Christ over, 51-
  59, 65

Enoch, book of, 56-57
Example of Christ. *See* Jesus
  Christ

Flavel, John, on counting the
  cost of committing to
  Christ, 75

Grace as more than unmer-
  ited favor, 60

Healing, the atonement and,
  33

Jesus Christ
 death of, physical, 51-52
 death of, spiritual, 52
 example of, 13-39
 Shepherd of the church, 33-
  35
 sinlessness of, 16-18
 spirit of, 51-53
 substitutionary work of. *See*
  Substitution, doctrine of
 suffering of, 7-76. *See also*
  Suffering
 superstar mentality, 28
 supremacy of, 71-73
 triumph of, 37-76
 victory over demons. *See*
  Demons

Krummacher, F. W., on
  Christ's humiliation,
  22-23

Latimer, Hugh, martyrdom
  of, 21

Mass, the. *See* Catholicism
McCheyne, Robert Murray,
  on the benefit of suf-
  fering, 12

81

Mead, Matthew, on apparently suffering for Christ, 75
Morris, Leon, on Christ's substitutionary work, 26-28

Nephilim. *See* Demons, pre-Flood
Noah. *See* Ark

Occult, the. *See* Witchcraft
Overcomers, 35

Persecution. *See* Suffering
Pink, A. W., on grace, 60

Retaliation. *See* Revenge
Revenge, not seeking, 18-20, 35
Roman Catholicism. *See* Catholicism

Sacrifice, of Christ. *See* Atonement
Satanism. *See* Witchcraft
Sin, bearing. *See* Atonement
Spurgeon, Charles Haddon
  on the doctrine of substitution, 31-32
  on glory through suffering, 34
Stibbs, Alan
  on 1 Peter 2:23, 20
  on 1 Peter 3:21, 69
Substitution, doctrine of, 26-33. *See also* Atonement
Suffering
  avoiding, 12, 36
  benefits of, 9, 12, 34

call to, 8-9
for Christ, 74-76
of Christians, 15
of Christians vs. non-Christians, 12
contentment amidst, 46-47
example of Christ's, 11-39
fairness of Christ's, 27-28
glory through, 7-12, 34
God's will and, 15
identification with Christ in, 10-11
reason for, 8-9, 12, 34-35, 74
responding to, 16-23, 73-74
sin and, 36
triumph of Christ's, 37-76

Tartarus, 56-57
Tozer, A. W., on letting fear keep us quiet, 23
Triumph, suffering and. *See* Suffering

Van Ryn, August, on 1 Peter 3:21, 70
Vengeance. *See* Revenge
Victory
  over demons. *See* Demons
  suffering and. *See* Suffering
Vine, W. E., on 1 Peter 3:18, 42

Watson, Thomas
  on being a favorite of God's, 47
  on sin vs. suffering, 36
Wesley, Charles, "And Can It Be That I Should Gain," 60-61
Witchcraft, perverted sex and, 65